Where We Live

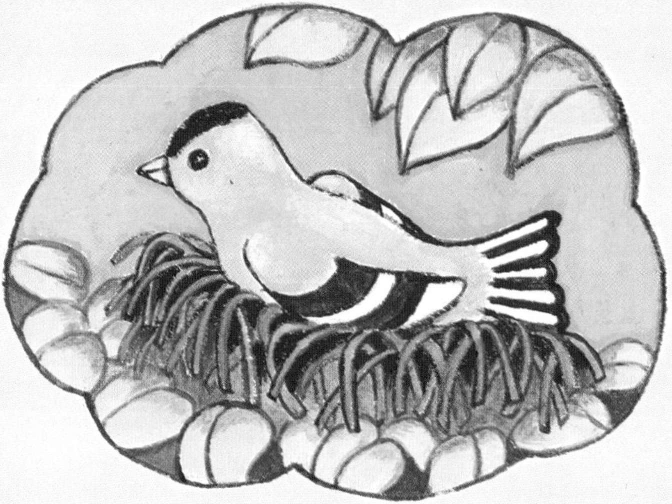

by Brad Necrason
illustrated by Freddie Levin

Harcourt
Orlando Boston Dallas Chicago San Diego

www.harcourtschool.com

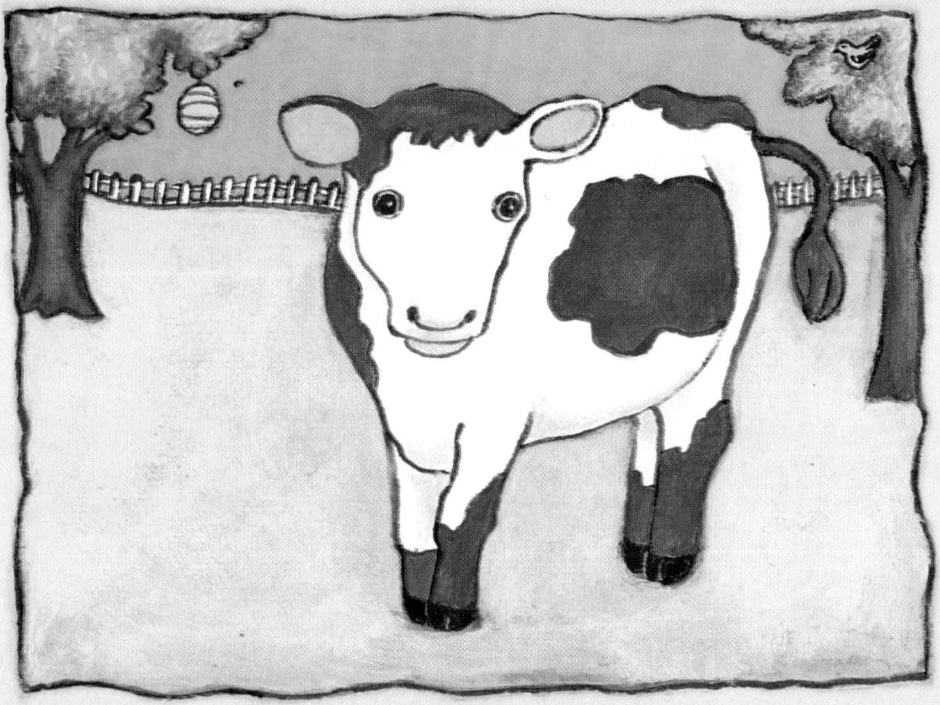

the cow

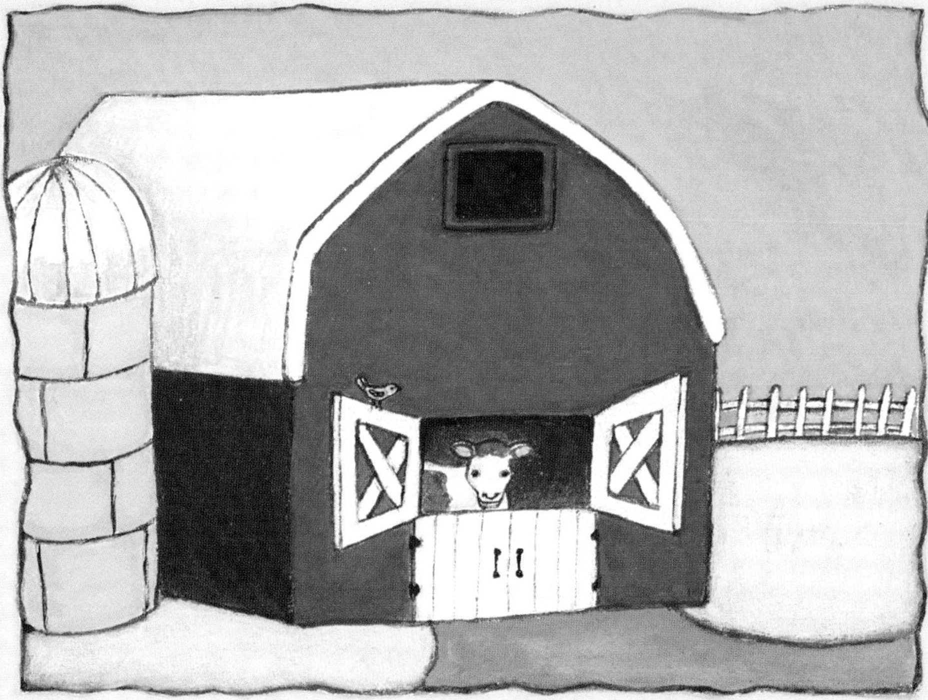

the barn

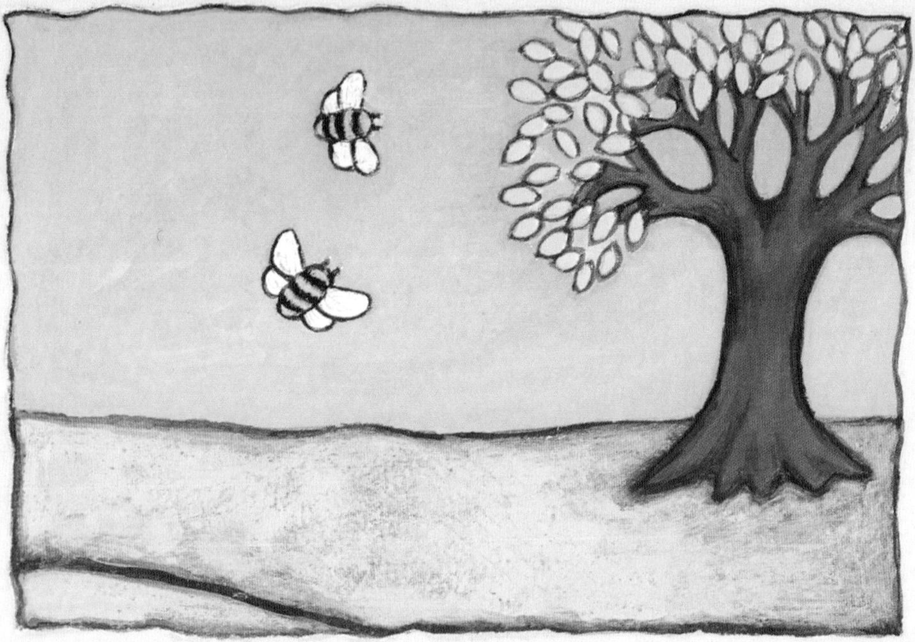

the bees

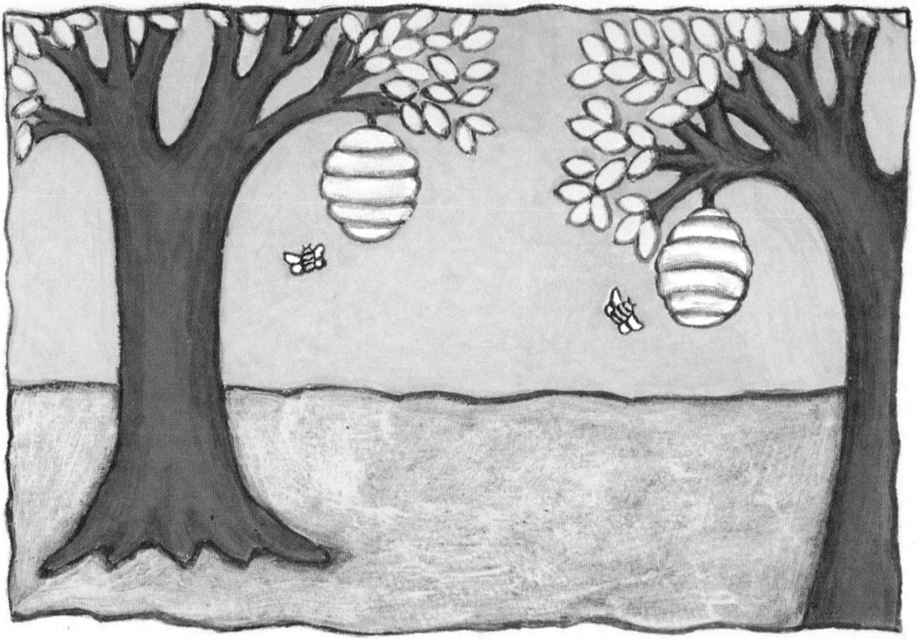

the hives

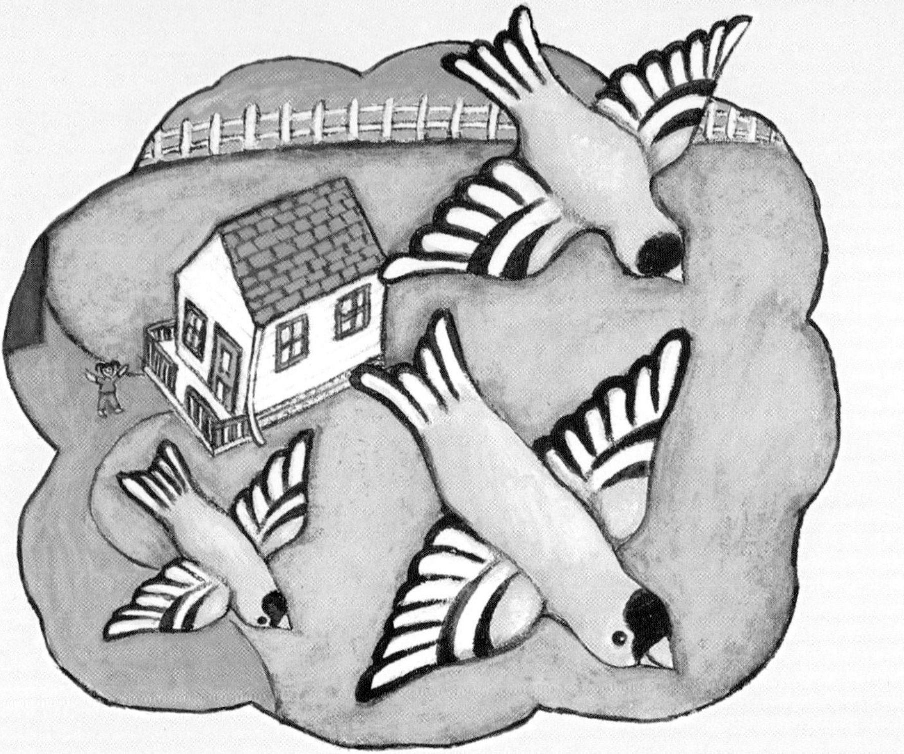

the birds

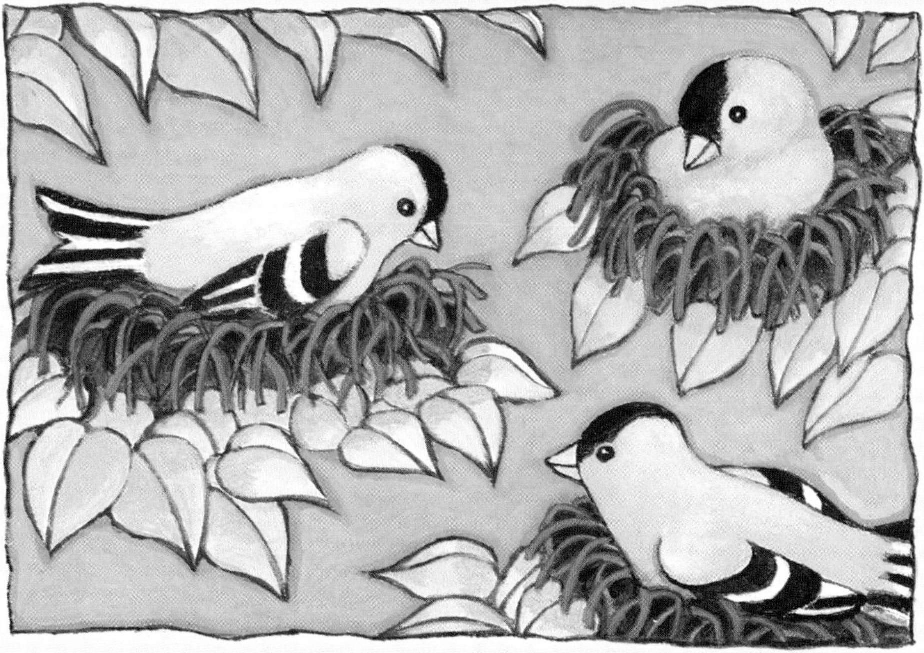

the nests

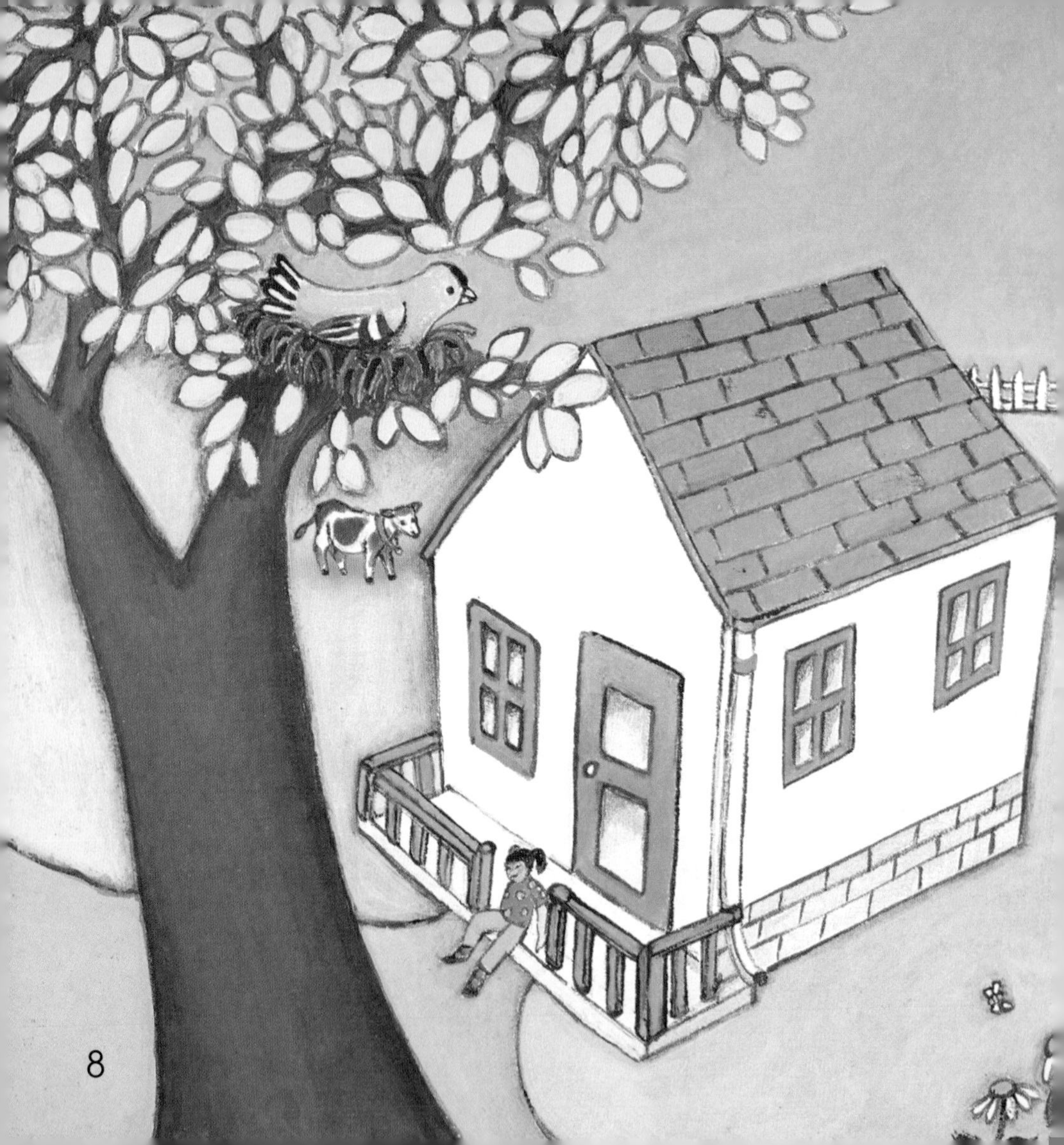